M000305778

IMAGES
of America

LOS ANGELES'S
HISTORIC BALLPARKS

IMAGES
of America

LOS ANGELES'S
HISTORIC BALLPARKS

Chris Epting

ARCADIA
PUBLISHING

Published by Arcadia Publishing
Charleston, South Carolina

Library of Congress Control Number: 2009937655

For all general information contact Arcadia Publishing at:
Telephone 843-853-2070
Fax 843-853-0044
E-mail sales@arcadiapublishing.com
For customer service and orders:
Toll-Free 1-888-313-2665

Visit us on the Internet at www.arcadiapublishing.com

*This book is dedicated to Tom Duino, John Outland, and
Richard Wojcik, who generously shared many of their
personal treasures to make this book more special than
I ever could have imagined. Thank you, men.*

CONTENTS

ACKNOWLEDGMENTS

I would like to thank the following people for their generosity in allowing me to use their photographs for this book: the Catalina Island Museum, the A.F. Gilmore Company, *Los Angeles Herald-Examiner* archive, Tom Meigs, Tom Duino, Richard Wojcik, and John Outland. As well, special thanks as always go to Jean, Charlie, and Claire, the best family in the world. They also go to my mom for always believing in me. And thanks are deserved by all of the great researchers, writers, and documentarians, including Richard Beverage, the folks at the Society for American Baseball Research (SABR), baseball-fever.com, ballparks.com, and Terry Cannon from The Baseball Reliquary (among others)—for all of your hard work over the years. You make projects like this easier, and more fun. Finally, thank you to Jerry Roberts, Devon Weston, Scott Davis, Kai Oliver-Kurtin, Julie Rivers, Lynn Beahm, and the rest of the team at Arcadia Publishing for their continued professionalism and hard work—as always, this was a pleasure.

INTRODUCTION

When most people think of professional baseball in the Los Angeles area, the Dodgers and Angels first come to mind. After all, the Dodgers have played in L.A. since 1958, and the Angels became part of Major League Baseball (MLB) in 1961, after thriving as a Pacific Coast League (PCL) team from 1903 to 1957. But of course, the history of professional baseball around Los Angeles is a much deeper one—as are the stories of the ballparks associated with that history.

Many fans can remember the Dodgers playing at the Los Angeles Memorial Coliseum in their first few years out west before their jewel, the vaunted Dodger Stadium, opened in 1962. The Coliseum, with its football-friendly layout, boasted some of the oddest configurations in baseball history. But it was here that many locals first experienced Major League Baseball.

Then there was the original Wrigley Field near downtown Los Angeles. It was called "Wrigley" before that other park in Chicago, and it's where the Angels played for decades as a PCL team and then for the first year after joining the majors in 1961. In addition to all of the Angels games played at Wrigley, the ballpark was a virtual soundstage, featured in many movies over the years. It substituted for both Yankee Stadium *and* Sportsman's Park in *Pride of the Yankees*. *Damn Yankees* was also one of the many other movies shot here. Television featured the park in the classic *Twilight Zone* episode "Mighty Casey," and the syndicated 1960 series *Home Run Derby* was also shot here.

In Hollywood, Gilmore Field (located near the Farmer's Market from the 1930s through the 1950s), hosted a galaxy of celebrities who liked baseball (and fans who liked to star-gaze). The Hollywood Stars of the PCL were beloved in the city, and even today PCL fans and players gather throughout the area to reminisce about that golden era of baseball.

Those are the places you may have heard about, but there are more ballparks to the story. There was the turn-of-the-century Chutes Park in Los Angeles, which was part of an amusement park. There was Olive Memorial Stadium in Burbank (where the St. Louis Browns would come for spring training), Brookside Park in Pasadena, and still another Wrigley Field on Catalina Island, where the Cubs trained for some 30 years. There are still other diamonds in the dust scattered throughout Orange and Riverside counties, where legends including Babe Ruth, Joe DiMaggio, Connie Mack, and many others appeared, and you will find them all in this book.

Angels (formerly Anaheim) Stadium in Anaheim is also included. Since it opened in 1966, the stadium has undergone not one but two major overhauls. And while many fans around the country may not consider "The Big A" a classically historic field, consider this: as of this writing, it is the fourth-oldest ballpark in use today in the major leagues—right behind Dodger Stadium, now the third-oldest. (Fenway Park in Boston and Chicago's Wrigley Field are, of course, the first- and second-oldest MLB parks still in use.)

In addition to photographs from my personal collection, in this book you'll be treated to some stunning and rare images from several generous individuals. In several cases, these images are being presented publicly for the first time; I hope they take your breath away as they did mine. Joe DiMaggio at Wrigley Field, Walter Johnson and Babe Ruth at the old Brea Bowl—I still cannot believe my good fortune in being able to include many of these pictures in this book.

The L.A. area may not be able to claim the well-known baseball history of the East Coast, but it does boast many notable stadiums big and small, where regional and national legends made plenty of history. Even today, kids out here on the West Coast play baseball year-round in sandlots, on Little League diamonds, and on every surface in between, in some cases on the very spots where the game's greatest legends once roamed in the California sun.

Some of the L.A. area's historic baseball places have markers; some are still standing, and some have been completely stripped of all former glory. This book is about to visit them all right now, from the famous jewels to the forgotten gems.

One

ANGELS, MOVIES, AND THE BABE

Wrigley Field—Los Angeles

The back of this postcard depicting Wrigley Field in the 1930s declares it as "Finest on the West Coast." Built in 1925 for $1.3 million at Forty-second Place and Avalon Avenue (about a mile east of the Los Angeles Memorial Coliseum), Wrigley Field was home to the Los Angles Angels of the PCL from 1925 to 1957, and the American League Los Angeles Angels in 1961. The stadium was originally owned by the Chicago Cubs, and it was designed to be like Cubs' Park (which was renamed for owner William Wrigley Jr. the following year). L.A.'s Wrigley Field stood until 1969.

Baseball great George Herman "Babe" Ruth is seen here in a still from the 1932 film *Fancy Curves*, which was shot in part at Wrigley Field. Wrigley would become a popular location site for future Hollywood baseball movies and television shows. In fact, Babe would return here to play himself in the classic Lou Gehrig biography *The Pride of the Yankees*.

This is another still from 1932's *Fancy Curves*, featuring Babe Ruth as he taught a team of female players the skills of baseball. Over the years, dozens of movies and television shows were shot here, including the films *It Happens Every Spring*, *Damn Yankees*, *Angels in the Outfield*, and television's popular *Home Run Derby*.

Babe Ruth leaps into home during a 1920s exhibition game at Wrigley Field. Wrigley's distinctive architecture (at left) makes it an easy park to identify, even with such a scant portion of it showing.

Before an Angels-Sacramento Solons game in 1942, Angels president Clarence Rowland tells soldiers the story behind the famed Wrigley Field Memorial Tower, erected to honor soldiers of World War I. Baseball games in the PCL in those years were used to raise money for the Army-Navy baseball equipment fund. From left to right are Carl Moore, Dean Patterson, Cpl. Charles Greenwald, Rowland, Gordon Ogilvie, and Ted Parker. I owe a special thanks to baseball writer Tom Hoffarth for this piece of research.

In this postcard view of Wrigley Field, Commissioner Kenesaw Mountain Landis delivers the dedication address as the stadium's renowned memorial tower is dedicated on January 15, 1926.

In this 1930 view, it's easy to see the letters spelling out W-R-I-G-L-E-Y F-I-E-L-D on the clock face of the stadium's landmark tower, which was visible for miles round Los Angeles.

Wrigley Field— Finest Ball Park On Pacific Coast

There were 23,083 persons at beautiful Wrigley Field the afternoon of this game between the Angels and the San Diego Padres.

How To Get There

Located at 42nd Place and Avalon Blvd., about a mile east of the Coliseum.

By automobile—Wrigley Field is just a few short blocks from the Harbor Freeway. Leave the Freeway at Santa Barbara Ave. and turn right. You can spot the park easily because of the 12-story high Memorial Tower and the block square grandstand and playing field.

By Street Car—Board the "S" car downtown going east on 7th Street between Grand and San Pedro. Leave car at 42nd Place. Board the "V" car going south on Vermont Ave. It turns east on Vernon to Avalon.

By Bus—Coach Line 4, running south from downtown.

When Built and the Tower

Wrigley Field was built in 1925 and the first game was played on Sept. 29, 1925, when the Angels defeated San Francisco, 10 to 8, before 18,000 persons.

The cost of construction was more than a million dollars in 1925, and the estimated replacement cost is obviously several times more than that now.

The Memorial Tower was built in honor of heroes of World War I by Mr. William Wrigley, Jr., and was dedicated Jan. 15, 1926, by the late Judge Landis, then commissioner of baseball. The Tower is 150 feet high.

Improvements

Wrigley Field is in its third year of a five-year improvement plan when another $50,000 was spent to give patrons the best in comfort and pleasant surroundings.

The box seat sections have been enlarged by more comfortable form-fitting seats installed by the American Seating Co. of Grand Rapids, Mich., whose years of experience have produced the utmost in comfortable seating. Soft foam rubber cushions, manufactured by Cobro Foam Sales of Los Angeles, are attached to the seats, eliminating the necessity of buying a cushion.

A new box office on the ground floor for future game tickets.

A new concession stand for the convenience of people in the upper deck has been constructed.

An improved ticket control in the re-modeled entrance will afford immediate entry into the park.

Miscellaneous

The scoreboard, one of the best in baseball, was remodeled in 1940, and again this year it has been epecially adapted for daytime ball. There are 537 lights used to make this highly informative board operate. It is 72 feet long, 50 feet high (including bleachers height) and five feet wide.

Do grass sprinklers at home bother you? There are 265 sprinklers in Wrigley Field and they spout four million gallons of water per season.

The first night game was played in Wrigley Field on July 22, 1934, and the Angels won from Sacramento, 5 to 4, in 11 innings.

Wrigley Field, Pacific Coast League Attendance Records

ONE DAY *

ANGELS — 23,497, against Hollywood, Aug. 7, 1952 (single game).
LEAGUE — 23,603, San Francisco against Oakland, July 30, 1946 (single game).

ONE SERIES

ANGELS — 79,241, against Hollywood, Sept. 9-14, 1930, (seven games). For eight games, 91,384, against Hollywood, Aug. 24-30, 1953. For nine games, 95,387, against San Francisco, June 29-July 5, 1948.
LEAGUE — 111,622, San Francisco against Oakland, July 30-Aug. 4, 1946. (Seven game series, but separate morning and afternoon games on Sunday, one game in each city).

ONE SEASON

ANGELS — 623,072, plus 36,124 in playoffs, 1947.
LEAGUE — 670,563, San Francisco, in 1946.

*Additional one-day records(Wrigley Field only):
Angels vs. San Diego, May 15, 1949 (Sunday doubleheader), 23,083.
Angels vs. San Francisco, Sept. 29, 1947, (playoff for pennant), 23,011.
Angels vs. Hollywood, Sept. 6, 1933, 22,746.
Angels vs. San Francisco, June 6, 1947, (Sunday doubleheader), 22,376.

Capacity

Box Seats	8,196
Grandstand	11,023
Bleachers	2,000
	21,219

Fence Distances, Height

Left Field	340 feet
Center Field	412 feet
Right Field (to screen)	338 feet, 6 in.
Right Field (to brk. wall)	346 feet, 7 in.

Height of wall, left field to centerfield corner— 14 feet, 6 inches. Height of wire screen, centerfield to right field—9 feet. Home plate to back stop—56 feet.

40

A page from the 1956 Los Angeles Angels yearbook details the stadium's history, stats, and amenities.

Here is the cover of the 1956 Los Angeles Angels yearbook. Players on this team included local legend Steve Bilko and Gene Mauch, who would go on to manage four major league teams (including the Angels, twice, in the 1980s).

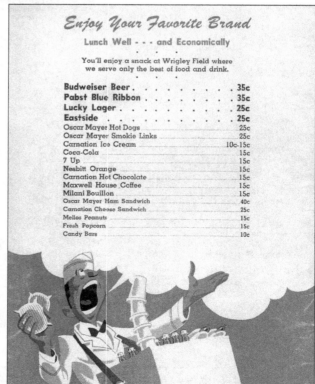

The back of the 1956 yearbook featured the stadium's food and drink menu, including 25¢ hot dogs and 25¢ and 35¢ beers.

NEWEST AND FINEST IN THE UNITED STATES

The caption on the back of this postcard reads, "Originally a Pacific Coast League park and the site of TV's *Home Run Derby*, Wrigley hosted the Angels only in 1961." A major league record was set that season for most homers hit in one park (245). Designed in the classic art deco style, the red-roofed white facade of the park resembled many of the park's surrounding homes. Seating just 20,500, Wrigley featured outfield fences that angled slightly toward home plate as they moved away from the foul lines, creating short power alleys and more home runs.

This image comes from a game played at Wrigley on July 21, 1951, against the PCL San Diego Padres. Note the empty upper deck.

15

This image, also from the July 21, 1951, games versus the Padres, features a broad view of the Wrigley Field grandstand on the third-base side.

A Padres batter takes a cut at a game versus the Angels at Wrigley Field on July 22, 1951. The right field stands (with an empty upper deck) are visible in this shot taken from the photographer's well in the third-base-side dugout.

It's time for some "Girls Softball Practice," as it was documented on the negatives of these images shot at Wrigley Field on April 6, 1949. The teams from the nearby cities of Monrovia and Buena Park practiced in the empty stadium this day. Wrigley was used by a myriad of local teams and groups throughout its history.

In a shot that appears to date from the early 1960s, the Westminster Neighborhood Association Wildcats prepare for a football game at Wrigley Field.

The call appears to be "out" at second on August 5, 1951, with the Oakland Oaks of the PCL visiting the Los Angeles Angels. Note how close the buildings beyond the outfield wall are to the park—literally just across the street.

It's September 2, 1951, and the Hollywood Stars have made the short trip to Wrigley for a cross-town game. In this shot, Angel Dee Fondy is caught in a pickle between second and third base in the first inning. Note the ivy-covered walls, just like Wrigley's counterpart stadium in Chicago.

Workers in the late 1940s maintain the ivy on the outfield wall of Wrigley Field. Like the other Wrigley Field, in Chicago, the brick outfield walls were covered with the distinctive greenery.

In addition to sporting events, Wrigley Field was also home to many other important community events. This image is from a 1963 "Freedom Rally" where Dr. Martin Luther King Jr. spoke to 35,000 people. As writer Tom Hoffarth points out, "A story a couple of weeks later in the *Herald-Examiner* read: 'Two weeks ago when Los Angeles Negroes massed at Wrigley Field, the signal was sounded for equal rights fight.' "

On May 18, 1956, Sugar Ray Robinson fought Carl "Bobo" Olson for the middleweight title, and won. This interesting angle was taken from the upper deck down the left field line at Wrigley Field.

20

This beautiful exterior shot of Wrigley Field was taken in December 1960. The next season, the field would see its one year of Major League Baseball as home to the Los Angeles Angels.

In 1957, owner Walter O'Malley traded his farm club, the Fort Worth Cats, for the Los Angeles Angels and Wrigley Field. This transaction gave O'Malley territorial rights to Los Angeles, and with it, plans for a new Dodger Stadium somewhere in Los Angeles. Many in the city figured O'Malley would slide the Dodgers over to Wrigley Field, and so architects drafted this view of the stadium, which illustrated how seating capacity would be boosted. These plans were never realized.

Before the start of the 1951 major league season, the New York Yankees embarked on a West Coast barnstorming tour, which matched them against the Los Angeles Angels, the Hollywood Stars, Sacramento Solons, Oakland Oaks, and San Francisco Seals. This was the final year of Joe DiMaggio's illustrious career and the first for a 19-year-old rookie named Mickey Mantle, so when the team pulled into Wrigley Field, it was a special event. The following rare images from the game, like this one of manager Casey Stengel at home plate, are treasures. They are the property of baseball aficionado Tom Duino, and I am deeply thankful for his generosity.

Joe DiMaggio, in his last year of Major League Baseball, bats at Wrigley Field during an exhibition game versus the Angels in March 1951.

The New York Yankees warm up at Wrigley Field in March 1951.

Yankee pitcher Tommy Byrne (28) hits some fielding practice at Wrigley in 1951. Note the outfield ivy and the close proximity of houses just beyond the outfield wall. It was a common occurrence for home run balls to break windows and land in the yards of these houses along East Forty-first Place.

Joe DiMaggio is seen outside the Yankee dugout at the Yankees-Angels exhibition game in March 1951. To the right of Joltin' Joe is another fading light, four-time All-Star first baseman Tommy Heinrich, who would not make the team that year, and would eventually retire after being traded to the St. Louis Browns.

This beautiful shot of the Yankees warming up before the game was shot from the first-base-side box seats at Wrigley Field.

Yankee shortstop Phil Rizzuto takes his turn at bat at Wrigley Field. This same year, 1951, Rizzuto met a young blind boy named Ed Lucas, who had lost his sight when he was struck by a baseball between the eyes on October 3 (the same day that the New York Giants' Bobby Thomson hit his famous "Shot Heard 'Round the World" home run). Rizzuto took an interest in the boy and the school the boy attended, St. Joseph's School for the Blind. Until his death, Rizzuto raised millions of dollars for St. Joseph's by donating profits from his commercials and books, and also by hosting the Annual Phil Rizzuto Celebrity Golf Classic and "Scooter" Awards. (Note the photographers on the field near the Angel dugout.)

This shot of Joe DiMaggio also provides a good view of the right-field grandstand at Wrigley Field.

25

Another rare collection of Wrigley Field images, these from Picture Day in 1961, when fans were allowed to meet the and photograph Angel players before the game, were graciously provided by Richard Wojcik, whose collection of vintage slides is beyond impressive. Here, in the background, Angels players sign autographs while others practice nearby. (Thanks to Richard Wojcik for this set of images.)

A young fan gets a prized Angels autograph. This image, shot near home plate, provides a good view of the outfield scoreboard. (Note the halo on the old-fashioned Angels cap.)

More players are seen on the field in the pregame meet and greet.

Pitcher Ryne Duren (left) and slugger Steve Bilko (right) warm up before the game. Note the detail of the Wrigley Field upper deck. Duren was known for his fastball but was also noted for his very poor vision and thick glasses. Legend has it that Duren once hit a player in the on-deck circle because he could not see which way to throw to home plate. Bilko slugged the club's first MLB home run, and was the first player to play for both the Los Angeles Dodgers and the American League Angels.

Angels manager Bill Rigney signs an autograph for a young fan. An eight-season major league veteran as an infielder, Rigney followed up his playing career by serving as Giants manager from 1956 to 1960, which included the team's first season after moving from New York to San Francisco in 1958. In 1961, he became the Angels' first manager, won the AL Manager of the Year Award in 1962, moved with them to Anaheim in 1966, and remained at the helm until midway through the 1969 season.

This image was taken behind the railing near the Angels dugout during a 1961 game against the Boston Red Sox.

Above, Angels star
Lee Thomas signs an
autograph book. Primarily
a first baseman for the
1961–1964 Angels, Thomas
also played in the outfield.

At right is another fan
image from the Angels'
first Picture Day in 1961.

The Angels' legendary first baseman, Steve Bilko, is seen here at Wrigley Field. Bilko's greatest year came in 1956 when he won the PCL's Triple Crown, hitting with a .360 batting average, 55 HR, and 164 RBI.

Two

MOVIE STARS AND THE HOLLYWOOD STARS

Gilmore Field at 7700 Beverly Boulevard in Los Angeles was home to the Hollywood Stars of the PCL from 1939 until 1957, when they and the Los Angeles Angels were displaced by the transplanted Brooklyn Dodgers of the National League. The stadium had a seating capacity of 12,987 and was a haven for movie stars and other celebrities throughout the life of the park.

This stunning aerial shot features Gilmore Stadium (left) and Gilmore Field (right). Gilmore Stadium was a multipurpose stadium opened in May 1934 and demolished in 1952, when the land was used to build the CBS Television City. The stadium held 18,000 and was the site where midget car racing was invented, as well as the home field for the Los Angeles Bulldogs of the American Football League (1936–1947). The Hollywood Stars also played here while they were waiting for Gilmore Field to be built. The stadium and field were both erected by Earl Gilmore, son of Arthur F. Gilmore and president of A. F. Gilmore Oil, a California-based petroleum company that was developed after Arthur struck oil on the family property.

This 1953 Hollywood Stars scorecard features Jodie "Red Fury" Munger on the cover.

The interesting 1953 view below gives a sense of how close Gilmore Field was to the Los Angeles Farmers Market. The market, then comprised of a series of clapboard buildings, can be seen at the photograph's center. The stadium is just left of center.

This 1950s postcard shows Gilmore Field. On the night the park opened, May 2, 1939, stars Jack Benny, Al Jolson, Gary Cooper, Robert Taylor, Bing Crosby, and starlet and co-owner Gail Patrick (wife of Brown Derby-owner Bob Cobb) were all on hand for the festivities. Although L.A.'s Wrigley Field received lots of Hollywood screen time, Gilmore Field also had its moments. It was featured in a 1949 movie called *The Stratton Story*, starring James Stewart and June Allyson, the true story of White Sox pitcher Monte Stratton, whose career was curtailed due to a hunting accident.

This split postcard features both Gilmore Field's interior and its exterior.

Gilmore Field, under construction, is seen from Third Street in Los Angeles, with the Hollywood Hills visible in the background.

An aerial shot shows Gilmore Field shortly after it opened in 1939. The field had intimate quarters for spectators: first and third bases were just 24 feet from the first row of seats. Home plate was 34 feet from the stands. In 1948, Gilmore Field became the spring training location for the Pittsburgh Pirates.

Gilmore Field is seen from deep center field. Baseball legends who played for the Hollywood Stars included longtime-PCL spitball ace Frank Shellenback, future Red Sox legend Bobby Doerr, Brooklyn-Dodger-great Babe Herman, MLB Hall-of-Famer Bill Mazeroski, and Joe DiMaggio's older brother, Vince.

The photograph captures Opening Day at Gilmore Field, May 2, 1939.

Preserved here is an image from a Hollywood Stars and San Francisco Seals game, played on July 29, 1951.

Another image from the above-mentioned Stars-Seals game features a good view of the third-base grandstands at Gilmore Field.

PACIFIC COAST LEAGUE HISTORICAL SOCIETY
GILMORE FIELD AND THE HOLLYWOOD STARS

A COMMEMORATION
SEPTEMBER 7, 1997

A
CENTURY
OF
BASEBALL
1839 - 1939

HOLLYWOOD STARS

OFFICIAL
PROGRAM

Welcome to the
STAR'S
First Home

Gilmore Field

10 ¢

OPENING DAY PROGRAM——MAY 2, 1939

The Gilmore Field site was abandoned after 1957, and the park was razed in 1958. Today much of the site is occupied by a parking lot at CBS Television City, near the Farmers Market. On September 7, 1997, the Pacific Coast League Historical Society, CBS, and the A. F. Gilmore Company dedicated a bronze plaque in commemoration of Gilmore Field on a wall outside CBS Studio 46.

Below, the author's son, Charlie, attends the Gilmore Field plaque dedication on September 7, 1997.

Three

FROM RIDICULOUS
TO SUBLIME

Shown here on Opening Day for the Los Angeles Dodgers in 1958, the Coliseum was clearly not built for baseball. Note the huge foul territory near third base, and the lack of it behind first.

Southern California took to the Dodgers right away, and many games were packed, like this 1959 contest, despite the insane distances that one might have to sit from the action. The Dodgers hosted the All-Star Game and three World Series games here in 1959. Attendance exceeded 92,000 for each World Series game, and the attendance of 92,706 for Game Five is still a MLB record. In only their second year in Southern California, the Dodgers won the 1959 World Series.

On Opening Day, comedian Joe E. Brown (center) introduces Dodger skipper Walter Alston (right). Giants and future Angels manager Bill Rigney looks on. The Dodgers won, 6-5, before a crowd of 78,672.

The Dodgers take batting practice, 1958. This view from right-center gives an idea of what it looked like to play the Coliseum outfield—quite a difference from cozy Ebbets Field in Brooklyn.

The legendary left-field fence at the Coliseum is seen in 1958. Due to the unusually short distance to left field (just 251 feet), a 42-foot-high screen was erected in an attempt to reduce the number of pop-fly home runs. Nonetheless, left-handed Dodgers outfielder Wally Moon intentionally hit pop flies to the opposite field—easy home runs in the Coliseum, screen or no screen. These became known as "moon shots."

The "3 a.m. Plan" had its peculiarities. The plan's name referred to Walter O'Malley's lack of sleep as he struggled with where the Los Angeles Dodgers would play that year. With moveable screens and fences, it was possible to configure the football field into a peculiarly shaped baseball field.

It's the top of the sixth inning of Game Four in the 1959 World Series between the Dodgers and the Chicago White Sox. As the scoreboard indicates, the attendance is 92,550: a new World Series record—until the next game, when the record would be broken again.

This ground-level view from 1959 gives you an idea of the broad expanse on which baseball was played in the Coliseum.

METROPOLITAN LOS ANGELES
The Story of The Los Angeles Memorial Coliseum and The Los Angeles Memorial Sports Arena

This late-1950s magazine cover shows how close the Coliseum is to the Los Angeles Memorial Sports Arena, seen at the upper right. Notice the seats under the scoreboard in right-center field. They were about 700 feet from home plate.

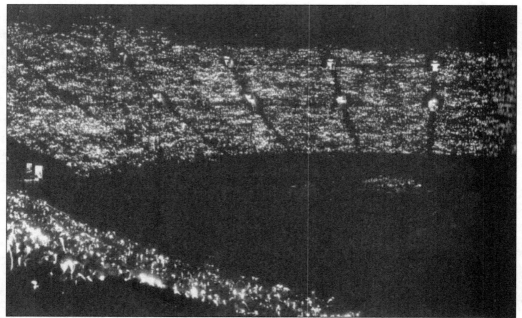

Roy Campanella Night was held at the Coliseum on May 7, 1959. Four months before the Dodgers opened in Los Angeles, the team's beloved catcher Roy Campanella was paralyzed in a car accident. A year later, the Dodgers and Yankees (in an exhibition game) drew 93,103 people to the Los Angeles Coliseum to honor Campanella—making it, for many years, the largest crowd ever for a major-league game. In a pregame ceremony, Campanella was wheeled out to second base by his longtime teammate, shortstop Pee Wee Reese. The Coliseum's lights were turned off, and the fans lit matches to greet him.

On March 29, 2008, to commemorate the 50h anniversary of the Dodgers arriving at the Coliseum, an exhibition game was played between the Dodgers and the Boston Red Sox. The Sox beat the Dodgers 7-4 Saturday night before an announced crowd of 115,300—largest ever to watch a baseball game. (The previous record of about 114,000 attended an exhibition between the Australian national team and an American services team during the 1956 Melbourne Olympics.)

46

The Dodgers get an upgrade: Dodger Stadium. The ballpark was built from 1959 to 1962 at a cost of $23 million, paid for through private financing. Dodger Stadium is currently the third-oldest ballpark in Major League Baseball, behind Fenway Park in Boston and Wrigley Field in Chicago.

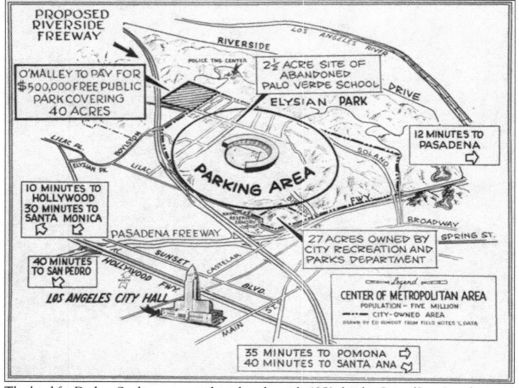

The land for Dodger Stadium was purchased in the early 1950s by the City of Los Angeles using eminent domain with funds from the Federal Housing Act of 1949. The city had planned to develop the Elysian Park Heights public housing project, which included two dozen 13-story buildings and more than 160 two-story townhouses, in addition to newly rebuilt playgrounds and schools. Those plans changed, however, when L.A. voters approved a "Taxpayers Committee for Yes on Baseball" referendum. This allowed the Dodgers to acquire 352 acres of Chavez Ravine from the city. This diagram of a proposed Dodger Stadium plan in Chavez Ravine is dated September 23, 1957, and it's very close to what was actually built.

This is a composite picture of the proposed Dodgers Stadium, dated March 13, 1958.

This *Herald-Examiner* newspaper caption on this photograph reads, "Chavez Ravine wrangle at City Council (Zoning), May 25, 1960. Map of Chavez Ravine—Dodger Stadium layout, roads, etc.; H. Douglas Brown (against zoning); John E. Roberts (City Planning Director) for zoning."

A splendid aerial view shows Dodger Stadium under construction on December 7, 1961.

The Dodger Stadium site is pictured as it looked during excavation on June 15, 1960.

On October 24, 1961, Dodger Stadium has begun to taken shape. It opened the next spring as home for both the Los Angeles Dodgers and the Los Angeles Angels. By 1966, the Angels had their own park in Anaheim.

Four

SMALL, STRANGE, AND OVERLOOKED

Chutes Park began in 1887 as a Los Angeles trolley park (a picnic and recreation area located at the end of or along streetcar lines). It was a 35-acre amusement park bounded by Grand Avenue on the west, Main Street on the east, Washington Boulevard on the north, and Twenty-first Street on the south. At various times it included rides, animal exhibits, a theater, and a baseball park. The Chutes ballpark was the original home of the PCL's Los Angeles Angels. This intriguing turn-of-the-century photograph shows the plunge ride; the ballpark (mostly out of frame) is located to the right of the plunge.

This incredible 1911 panorama shows Washington Park, which opened that year as the home park of both the Los Angeles Angels and the Vernon Tigers. Washington Park was built on part of the site previously occupied by Chutes Park, near the site of its baseball stadium. To the right

of center in the photograph, the water slide ride at the amusement park is visible. Washington Park remained in use through the end of the 1925 season.

Washington Park is seen around 1911. The picture's photonegative sleeve reads, "City Park. Chutes Park, adjoined, was privately owned."

Thirty-eighth Street and Santa Fe Avenue in Vernon was home of the short-lived Maier Park (also referred to as "Vernon Park") where the Vernon Tigers baseball team played until 1920, before moving over to Washington Park. (In between, the team spent some time playing in Venice, too). This image is of a 1911 boxing match held at Maier Park between Ad Wolgast and Joe Rivers. Wolgast prevailed.

Built in 1947, Olive Memorial Baseball Stadium in Burbank was located at Olive Avenue Park. In 1949, the City of Burbank entered into a contract with the St. Louis Browns for use of the Olive Avenue Memorial Stadium as a spring training headquarters. The St. Louis Browns opened spring training there in March 1949. The Browns played nine exhibition games, including two games against the 1948 World Champion Cleveland Indians. As many as 32,000 spectators attended the Browns games and practice sessions.

The St. Louis Browns came to be known as the "Burbank Browns." Each Sunday afternoon, the Burbank Browns played semiprofessional teams at the Olive Avenue Memorial Stadium. The Browns played here until 1952.

The image below shows how the outside of Olive Memorial looked in 1994, not long before it was torn down.

The author is seen visiting Olive Memorial shortly before it was razed in the mid-1990s.

The author's son, Charlie, "runs" to first base at Olive Memorial Stadium.

Removed by historian Chris Epting, and his two-year-old son Charlie (seen below), when Olive Memorial Stadium was being razed in the winter of 1994, this brick and dirt sample bear silent witness to Burbank's only brush with big league baseball . . . and to an era before Johnny Carson and Ed McMahon, when just a long home run from beautiful downtown Burbank, one could find Satchel Paige throwing his repertoire of baffling pitches to the likes of Luke Appling, Nellie Fox, Ralph Kiner, and Willie Mays. The brick and dirt are on loan from seven-year-old Charlie Epting, one of the youngest collectors of historic baseball artifacts in the country.

A portion of the 2001 exhibit hosted by The Baseball Reliquary is seen at left.

The view from home plate at Olive Memorial, below, looked off toward the San Gabriel Mountains.

The grandstand at Olive Memorial looked like this (above) just days before it was razed.

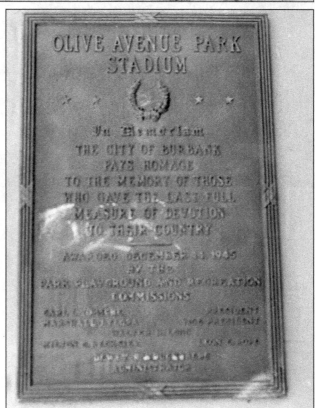

One of the plaques affixed to the outer stadium wall at Olive Memorial Stadium is seen at right.

This panorama of Olive Memorial was shot on the day the stadium was destroyed.

Some of the Olive Memorial artifacts from a 2001 display are seen here.

The exterior of the Olive Memorial Stadium grandstand is shown on the day that it was razed in the mid-1990s.

In 1912, the city of Pasadena acquired land for a small park in the arroyo. The site was originally known as the Sheep Corral Springs, as sheep from the San Gabriel Mission once grazed there. In 1914, Brookside Park was built here, in the shadow of the Rose Bowl. Six years later, the city hired architect Dorothy Schindler to design an amphitheater (Brookside Theater) on the hillside south of the Brookside Plunge. In 1932, Myron Hunt designed the stadium, dugouts, and adjoining clubhouse at Brookside Park Baseball Field (later renamed Jackie Robinson Memorial Field). The Chicago White Sox used Brookside as their spring training ground in 1933.

The diamond at Brookside Park is pictured here. Jackie Robinson played here, along with many other legends of the game.

A popular episode of *The Munsters* was filmed here featuring Leo Durocher and many of the Los Angeles Dodgers. The 1965 episode "Herman the Rookie" featured Herman (Fred Gwynne) trying out for—and making—the team.

Jackie Robinson, who grew up right near Brookside Park, is fondly remembered in his hometown of Pasadena.

Five

BASEBALL BY THE SEA

The Chicago Cubs trained on Catalina Island for many years (1922–1942, 1946 and 1947, and 1950 and 1951). Cubs owner William Wrigley Jr. bought a majority interest in the scenic island in 1919. The ballpark Wrigley built on the island featured the same dimensions as Wrigley Field in Chicago.

Wrigley Field on Catalina predated the Los Angeles minor league baseball facility of the same name, which didn't open until 1925. Additionally, this is technically the first baseball facility to bear Wrigley's name. The older park in Chicago was first called Weeghman Park, then Cubs Park, before being renamed Wrigley Field in 1926.

This 1925 image shows the Chicago Cubs posing with William Wrigley Jr. (in the white hat with his arms folded). Over the years, an incredible array of baseball stars spent their springs in the lush island setting, including Charlie Root, Phil Cavaretta, Charlie Grimm, and Hall of Famers Rogers Hornsby, Dizzy Dean, Gabby Hartnett, Joe McCarthy, Grover Cleveland Alexander, and Hack Wilson.

This image shows the 1933 team posing on the field. Each spring, the club would arrive aboard one of Wrigley's fleet of ships used for transportation from the mainland. Among these ships were the *Hermosa*, the *Cabrillo*, the SS *Avalon*, and the SS *Catalina*. Once gathered on the island, the players enjoyed all the creature comforts, including spending time at the elegant Hotel St. Catherine on Descanso Bay.

In this aerial view of Wrigley Field on Catalina Island, the small grandstand between home and first base is clearly visible.

The ballpark is long gone, but a clubhouse built by Wrigley to house the Cubs still exists as the Catalina County Club. By 1951, the team was finished with Catalina Island and training was moved to Mesa, Arizona. This modern image shows the remnants of the first-base grandstand. Note the supports jutting out of the hill.

An interesting aerial image shows Wrigley Field, Santa Catalina Island, around 1940.

For years, the historic memorial plaques that had once adorned the tower at Wrigley Field in Los Angeles were displayed in what would have been the deepest left-field corner of the ball field in Catalina. Here the author is pictured with his son near the plaques in 1992.

The author's daughter (foreground) and son and wife (background) are pictured at the former site of Catalina's Wrigley Field, looking from the site of the first-base-side grandstand.

Shell Field was Long Beach's first substantial baseball park, located at the northern foot of Signal Hill (today it's where the National Guard station is located at Redondo Avenue and Stearns Street). It was paid for by Shell Oil (this was an oil town after all), which fielded a team here. The Model

T Fords seen here were used to determine and enforce foul lines. Shell's oil derricks are prominent in the background of both photographs. (Courtesy of Tom Meigs/Chuck Stevens Collection.)

During the hot summer afternoons in Long Beach, Shell Field's grandstand's roof provided comfortable shade for baseball fans. Both of these photographs were taken on August 26, 1923,

during a game between Shell Oil and Union Oil. Note the wooden dugout roof in the lower-right corner of the photograph above. (Courtesy of Tom Meigs/Chuck Stevens Collection.)

Recreation Park, or "Rec Park," was built in 1924; this photograph shows it in 1939. The Dodgers, Los Angeles Angels, and Hollywood Stars played here as well as such Hall-of-Fame barnstormers as Satchel Paige, Cool Papa Bell, and Bob Feller. In 1958, Recreation Park was rededicated as Blair Field, in honor of local sports writing legend, Frank T. Blair. Newly renamed field opened on Friday, April 11, 1958 with Poly High School pitcher Gordon Nelson throwing the first pitch to Huntington Beach High School shortstop John Daros. Poly would win the game 3-1 before less than 100 fans. Four days later, Long Beach State would defeat Long Beach City College 14-6 in the park's first collegiate game. Ironically, the Los Angeles Dodgers and San Francisco Giants played their first "West Coast" game that same day. The author's children are pictured below at Recreation Park in 2001. (Courtesy of Tom Meigs.)

This shot of Blair Field was taken in 2001. In 1961, the Dodgers played an exhibition game at Blair Field versus the Dallas-Ft. Worth Rangers before a still-record 6,250 fans. In 1966, the Chicago Cubs held spring training and played eight exhibition games at the ballpark. The Angels and Indians played additional games there in 1967. For 13 years, the Los Angeles Rams used the facility as their practice site until their move to Anaheim.

In 2001, former major league catcher Steve Yeager came to Blair Field to manage the Long Beach Breakers in the (now defunct) Western Baseball League. He is pictured here with the author's children at Blaire Field, home field for the Breakers.

Six

OUTSIDE THE LINES

This rare image (from the aforementioned collection of Tom Duino) shows Anaheim Stadium in November 1965, about six months before the official opening. For many today, it is almost unfathomable that the area around the ballpark was once this wide open. There's some interesting science behind what would become the field's dimensions: The measurements (333 feet instead of 330, for example) were derived from a scientific study conducted by the Angels. Based on the air density at normal game times (1:30 p.m. and 8:00 p.m.), the Angels tried to formulate dimensions that were equally balanced between pitcher, hitter, and average weather conditions. The Angels adjusted these dimensions several times, searching for the proper balance.

Anaheim Stadium is pictured in November 1965. The Angels moved here from Dodger Stadium, where they had played since 1962.

Anaheim Stadium is seen here from a slightly different angle than in the above shot.

This construction photograph was taken in November 1964. Anaheim Stadium was built on a parcel of about 160 acres of flat farmland in southeast Anaheim.

Anaheim Stadium is seen as it looked during the 1967 All-Star Game in an image snapped from down the right field line.

The Angels took on the Minnesota Twins on April 23, 1966, right after Anaheim Stadium opened. The Big A scoreboard is clearly visible beyond the left wall. In 1967, the stadium hosted the MLB All-Star Game—the first to be played on national television.

The 1967 All-Star Game pregame festivities featured a Disneyland spectacular with singers and familiar characters.

Anaheim Stadium as it looked in December 1978. Disneyland is visible at the upper right, and the Anaheim Convention Center can be seen at top center.

Here is another shot from the 1967 All-Star Game at Anaheim Stadium. Tony Perez of the Cincinnati Reds homered off Catfish Hunter of the Kansas City Athletics in the 15th inning to break a 1-1 tie in the longest All-Star Game in history.

Fans in Anaheim Stadium enjoy the 1967 All-Star Game. Angels Manager Bill Rigney was coach in the game and the AL's roster included Angels Don Mincher, Jim Fregosi, and Jim McGlothlin.

This August 1980 image shows Anaheim Stadium after the renovations for football were completed. The Los Angeles Rams played here until 1995, when the team left California to become the St. Louis Rams.

Fans mill outside the stadium on April 23, 1966. The Angels finished 80-82 that year. These fans are also pictured on page 124 at the upper deck concessions on that day.

A fan stands near the Big A before the start of the 1967 All-Star Game. The stadium hosted the All-Star Game again in 1989 and 2010.

Built in the late 1930s as a spring training home for the PCL Seattle Rainiers, La Palma Park on Harbor Boulevard today is used for high school football, baseball, and soccer. In the 1940s, La Palma Park was the spring training base for the Philadelphia Athletics. Several years later, the St. Louis Browns trained there. Joe DiMaggio played here while stationed in nearby Santa Ana during World War II.

Here is La Palma Park (lower right) as it looked from the air in the 1940s. When Connie Mack brought his Philadelphia A's here in February 1940, the team stayed at the Angelina Hotel. Mack—who by this time had already managed the A's for 38 years— was quoted as saying, "This is the greatest set-up my club has ever had in a training camp."

The Philadelphia A's practice at La Palma Park in 1940. Some scenes from the movie *The Jackie Robinson Story* were filmed here in 1950, with Jackie Robinson playing himself.

The legendary Connie Mack meets with local youngsters during spring training in 1941.

This is a picture of Anaheim Union High School principal Joseph Clayes with Connie Mack at La Palma Park stadium during spring training in 1941.

Jimmie Heffron, *Anaheim Bulletin* sports editor, interviews Luke Sewell, manager of the St. Louis Browns, during spring training in March 1946 at La Palma Park.

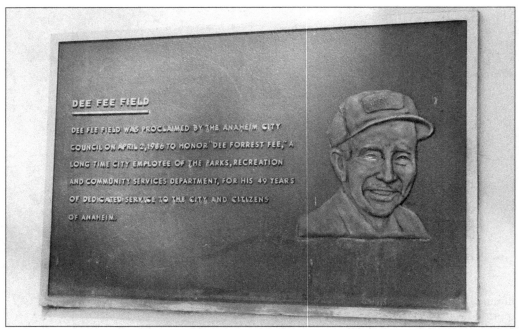

DEE FEE FIELD

DEE FEE FIELD WAS PROCLAIMED BY THE ANAHEIM CITY COUNCIL ON APRIL 2, 1986 TO HONOR "DEE FORREST FEE," A LONG TIME CITY EMPLOYEE OF THE PARKS, RECREATION AND COMMUNITY SERVICES DEPARTMENT, FOR HIS 49 YEARS OF DEDICATED SERVICE TO THE CITY AND CITIZENS OF ANAHEIM.

The stadium was dedicated to former Anaheim Union High School athletic director Richard M. Glover after his death in 1974. The baseball field was re-dedicated to local sports volunteer Dee Forrest Fee in 1986. Today a plaque on the outside of the stadium acknowledges Fee.

It may not be a ballpark, but it's a site that certainly figures into ballpark history and is included here simply for that reason. Within view of Angel Stadium of Anaheim at Melrose Abbey Memorial Park is the well-worn grave of Jack Norworth—the man who wrote "Take Me Out to the Ball Game." The 1908 classic was written on some scrap paper on a train ride to Manhattan, New York. Norworth then provided those paper scrap lyrics to Albert Von Tilzer, who composed the music, which in turn was published by the York Music Company. Before the year was over, a hit song was born. Born in Philadelphia, Norworth is credited as cowriter of a number of Tin Pan Alley hits, including "Shine On, Harvest Moon." Even though "Take Me Out to the Ball Game" was his most enduring hit, it was not until 1940 that he actually witnessed a baseball game. Norworth retired to Southern California and was living in Laguna Beach at the time of his death in 1959.

This 1929 aerial view of Anaheim City Park (now Pearson Park), located at 400 North Harbor Blvd., shows the Greek Theater at right, the "plunge" swimming pool and bathhouse at center (with tennis courts directly below), and the baseball field left of center. Used by many local teams (and sometimes by the teams visiting for spring training), the 1927 baseball field grandstand seated 750.

Baseball is being played at Pearson Park in the early 1930s.

The author pitches to his son at Pearson Park in 2001.

The author's son steps up to the plate at Pearson Park in 2001.

Fiscalini Field in San Bernardino was originally called Perris Hill Park. Through the years, the stadium was the spring training home of the Pittsburgh Pirates and St. Louis Browns, and was the home field for the San Bernardino Stars and the San Bernardino Pioneers. Stars including Honus Wagner (as a coach) and Ken Griffey Jr. (on his way up) played here.

Built in 1934 on the hill named for railroad developer Fredrick Thomas Perris, Perris Hill Park was renamed Fiscalini Field in 1993 after John Fiscalini, a San Bernardino native who earned All-Citrus Belt League baseball honors at San Bernardino High School, won All-American Laurel twice while playing at the University of California at Berkeley, and played professionally in the Pirates organization. Today the field is used primarily for college ball.

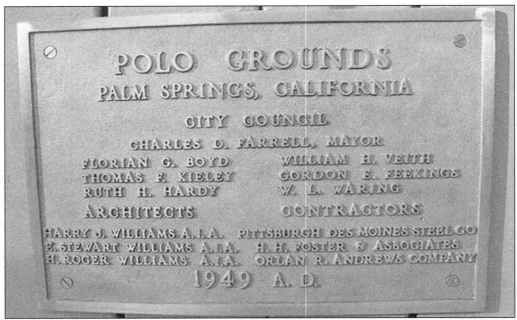

Farther south, in Palm Springs, is the Polo Grounds, built in 1949 for use by polo players. In 1960 when former Los Angeles Angels owner Gene Autry was awarded an American League expansion team, he made Palm Springs the team's spring training home. Later the stadium's name was changed to Angels Stadium, though the Angels, San Diego Padres, and Seattle Rainiers all shared the park during spring training.

The Los Angeles Angels train in Palm Springs in February 1961. Manager Bill Rigney watches over the exercising players. The AL franchise was known as the L.A. Angels from 1961 to midseason 1965, when it became the California Angels. From 1997 through 2005, when the Walt Disney Company owned the club, it was known as the Anaheim Angels. Since Arte Moreno took over the club in 2005, the team has been officially known as the Los Angeles Angels of Anaheim.

The Angels are seen at spring training in Palm Springs. Note the halos on top of the caps.

Amerige Park in Fullerton, opened in 1917, stands on the site of the old Fullerton High School. It was the spring training grounds for Pacific Coast League teams including the Hollywood Stars (1935–1936), Portland Beavers (1947–1950), Sacramento Solons (1941–1942 and 1944), and the Los Angeles Angels (1946–1955). Legends including Joe DiMaggio, Walter Johnson, and Satchel Paige all played here, and today Amerige Park (with a field named for Duane Winters, who served in city government for 26 years) is home to Fullteron's Little League Junior Division and Pony Colt League (and the original wooden stands have been replaced by concrete). In 1935, director Ray Enright brought his movie crew here from Hollywood to shoot a comedy called *Alibi Ike*, starring Joe E. Brown and Olivia de Havilland (the film was about a rookie pitcher for the Cubs who tormented his manager and fiancée with alibis and excuses for all of his strange habits.)

Babe Ruth [autograph]

On October 31, 1924, Babe Ruth and Walter Johnson played a barnstorming game in Brea that has become a solid part of the area's folklore. Sponsored by the Anaheim Elks Club, the game was a homecoming of sorts for Johnson, who grew up in the neighboring oil town of Olinda. A crowd of nearly 5,000 attended the game in Brea Bowl field, an incredible number given that nearby Anaheim's total population back then was just 2,000. Ruth's team won, 12-1, and the day was capped by two Ruth home runs, one of which supposedly traveled 550 feet. This game was documented by 18-year-old George E. Outland, who photographed baseball players as a hobby, and eventually got many of them to autograph the shots. (Outland became a delegate to the California State Democratic Conventions from 1942 to 1950, and was elected as a Democrat to the 78th and 79th U.S. Congresses.) Many thanks go to John Outland, George's son, for allowing these photographs to appear in this book.

Johnson's fellow Washington Senator Carl Sawyer is seen in Brea for the famous game. Today the site of the old Brea Bowl is a quiet neighborhood. Just two blocks away, at 227 North Brea Boulevard, there's an auto repair company. The old garage that still stands at the site is where all of the players got dressed for the game after getting off the train. From there, they marched down to the nearby field.

Hall-of-Famer Sam Crawford crosses the plate in Brea, met by none other than Babe Ruth.

This portrait shows George Outland on the right, posing with Sam Crawford.

The great Jimmie Austin poses for Outland. Note the autograph. George Outland spent time late in life tracing down players to have his photographs signed.

Rube Ellis poses for Mr. Outland. Ellis played for the St. Louis Cardinals from 1909 to 1912.

Sam Crawford poses near the makeshift backstop in Brea. Crawford, who played for the Cincinnati Reds early in his career, then many years for the Detroit Tigers, was inducted into the Baseball Hall of Fame in 1957.

Here is an incredibly rare image: Babe Ruth pitching in 1924! Though he had not thrown from the mound for years (he pitched for the Boston Red Sox before becoming a Yankee slugger), for this exhibition he made a special exception and thrilled the fans.

Here is another rare and precious image from the Outland Brea Collection. Babe Ruth crosses the plate after crushing one of his two monstrous home runs that day.

Local boy Walter Johnson poses for George Outland. Johnson later signed the photograph.

I NEVER SING IN PUBLIC!

ONLY TROJAN ENTHUSIAST WHO
LIFORNIA, HERE I COME," LAST
TRAIN LEFT FOR THE NORTH.

SPORTS
The LOS ANGELES Times

SATURDAY MORNING, NOVEMBER 1, 1924.

ERN CALIFORNIA FAVORED TO BREAK BEARS'

CHOOSIN' SIDES

Perhaps Walter Johnson and Babe Ruth used to do this when they were kids but, anyhow, they were caught in the act, not befitting for world's champs, just before they took part in a big exhibition game at Anaheim yesterday. Babe's side won the game.
[P. & A. Photo]

RUTH SWATS TWO HOMERS

IDAHO WINS OVER O. A. C.

Vandals Score Sensational 22 to 0 Victory Over Oregon Team in Game on Muddy Field

[BY A. P. NIGHT WIRE]

CORVALLIS (Or.) Oct. 31.—The University of Idaho today defeated the Oregon Agricultural College 22 to 0 in a game featured by passing and punting. The field was very muddy and there was scarcity of scrimmage play.

Idaho scored two touchdowns in the first period, both the result of a series of long passes by Stivers. Vesser scored the first touchdown and Stivers failed to convert. Following an exchange of kicks, Idaho took the ball on downs and Cameron carried the ball across for the second touchdown. Stivers kicked goal.

The game so far was mostly passing and punting with very little scrimmage.

Idaho opened up with another series of passes in the second period that quickly brought another touchdown, Vesser going across the goal line to receive the ball on the last play. Stivers failed to kick goal. The Aggies started a drive late in the period which brought the ball to Idaho's 26-yard

line with four long passes but the half ended before they could score.

Neither team scored in the third period during which the ball went back and forth with neither side getting a break. Idaho continued to play an open game. Near the end of the period, Idaho advanced the ball to the Aggies' 12-yard line, but Schulmerich intercepted a pass and carried the ball to his 20-yard line just before the period ended.

In the fourth period the ball went back and fourth mostly by passing, without a break until a few minutes before the end when Stivers made a place kick from the Aggies' 17-yard line. The place kick followed an exchange of punts and a fumble by O.A.C., which Idaho recovered on the Aggies' 26-yard line. A long pass

(Continued on Page 16, Column 6)

STATZ IS DEFEATED IN FINAL

Loses to Splendid Golf of Fuller Thompson at Griffith Park

GRID MENU
FOR TODAY

LOCAL.
Whittier at Occidental.
Local U.C. vs. Pomona at Claremont
Caltech at Redlands.
U.S.C. frosh vs. Cal. frosh at Coliseum.
Santa Ana J.C. at Loyola.
Pasadena A.C. vs. U.S.S. Penn-

TODAY'S LE

BY FE

ANDY SMITH.
FOOTBALL COACH.
UNIV. OF CALIFORNIA

OR THIS?

Above are the faces of two

The *Los Angeles Times* covered this now-legendary game.

Seven

SEARCHING
FOR THE PAST

The Los Angeles Coliseum is pictured here in 1958 with the Dodgers taking batting practice. The stadium is primarily used primarily for the University of Southern California Trojans football team.

Washington Park is pictured above around 1911. Today no trace of the park remains. It has been replaced by a technical school, seen below.

The image above shows Washington Park around 1915. The modern view below, taken from right field, reveals no trace today of what once stood in downtown Los Angeles. The park was razed in 1925.

Pictured above is the old slide ride at Chutes Park, located beside Washington Park. Nothing remains today.

The exterior of Gilmore Field is pictured above in the late 1930s. Today it is the site of the CBS Television City.

Gilmore Field was under construction in the mid-1930s. This view is from Third Street, with the Hollywood Hills in the background. Today the Grove Shopping Center blocks most of this view.

The tower and exterior of Wrigley Field is pictured above in May 1961, looking up East Forty-second Place. The ballpark was torn down in 1969; no part of it remains today.

Joe DiMaggio is pictured above at Wrigley Field in 1951. Though the stadium is gone, some of the houses remain beyond where the outfield wall once ran. A hospital occupies the Wrigley site today; the playing field would have been in the parking lot.

Another shot depicts the former field at Wrigley. A grassy area still remains in center field, as do some of the houses beyond the outfield wall.

The spot where Yogi Berra was interviewed on the field in 1961 is today a parking lot.

Another view, looking toward center field at Wrigley Field, is seen in both 1961 and 2009.

The view at Wrigley field looking toward left field is shown above in 1961 and below in 2009.

Dodger Stadium is pictured above as it looked on its very first opening day, April 10, 1962, when the Dodgers roster included Sandy Koufax, Don Drysdale, Maury Wills, and Tommy Davis. The image below was taken in the mid-1990s.

Wrigley Field at Catalina is pictured as it looked in the early 1940s.

Babe Ruth bats in this photograph taken on October 31, 1924, at the Brea Bowl.

In this modern view, the trees lining the field to the left still remain.

Today near St. Crispen Avenue, a car sits near where the Babe once stood.

Olive Memorial in Burbank, above, appears as it looked shortly before being torn down in the mid-1990s. The below shot was taken several weeks after it was razed.

A female fan is seen outside Anaheim Stadium in April 1966, which was opening week for the venue. Today, outside Gate 4, the dirt lot has been paved and the stadium has been remodeled—twice.

In the 1966 photograph above, four fans pose at a concession stand on the upper level of Anaheim Stadium near the entrance to section 427. Today very little has changed (except the prices).

The diamond at Anaheim Stadium is seen from the upper deck on April 23, 1966. Today a man-made mountain has been added just past center field and the Big A has been moved to an outer parking lot near the freeway.

Anaheim Stadium is seen in 1966, just several weeks after it opened. Today the Big A, visible in the "then" shot, stands in the outer parking lot.

The view above shows Anaheim Stadium in the early 1980s after it was enclosed for football. The modern view below was taken in 2009, 11 years after the refurbishment that returned the park to a semblance of its original, open design. Since the first photograph, the park's name had been changed to Edison International Field of Anaheim (1997), and then to Angel Stadium of Anaheim (2003).

Visit us at
arcadiapublishing.com

CPSIA information can be obtained
at www.ICGtesting.com
Printed in the USA
LVHW062249310720
662073LV00001B/158

9 781531 653132